4 Business Ideas to Generate an Online Income

Tried and Tested Practical Methods for Making Money Online in 2019

Steven MacRory BA

Contents

About This Book

The aim of this book is to clearly explain how to create an online income using 4, lesser known, proven systems that require little to no start-up capital. Covering the information and resources required to get started, this book is written in detailed yet clear and easy to understand language. The methods described are designed to be scalable, profitable, relatively easy, and none of them require stock or inventory.

The books explains each system, how it works, and how money can be made from it; advice and guidance on further learning if required; free and paid marketing ideas and systems for each particular method; expected start-up costs; the pros and cons of the system; and an easy to follow action plan to get the system up and running as quickly as possible.

Audience

This book is for anyone that would like to learn about ways to make money online with a small start-up budget. It is primarily aimed at people new to generating an online income that would like to get going quickly without the need to invest too much time or money. It may also assist people with some experience in making money online that are searching for new or additional methods to generate an income, or looking for new ideas to market their products or services.

Introduction

Around two years ago I began looking for ways to supplement my income. Coming from a computing background, the logical thing to do was to find ways of generating an income from my computer! I began reading e-books and doing lots of internet research. However, I found it very difficult to find anything that I was happy with. Much of the information seemed to point me in similar directions – selling on EBay or Amazon, completing surveys, starting my own website, and so on. None of them seemed concrete or scalable and they lacked the resources and advice that I really needed at that time. I also needed some honesty and guidance which is what I have attempted to provide in this book.

After lots of research, hard work, and time I have put the ideas presented in this book into practice. I am far from an overnight millionaire but the additional income generated by using these methods has really helped!

Remember that the main thing is to take action. Dedicate some time every day and don't give up when you hit hurdles. There has never been a better time to begin making money online. More people than ever are buying online, more people than ever are looking for online freelancers, and more people than ever need a website and an online presence.

Let's get started!

Start a Unique Online E-Commerce Store

Creating your own e-commerce store is a really exciting way to make money online. Here we shall cover how almost anyone can get their own unique brand up and running.

We shall go through the essentials of POD and what it is; the type of products you can sell and where to source them; how to generate ideas for your products; where and how to sell them; the costs of starting a POD business; the pros and cons of this type of business; and how to get started with a 'plan of attack'. The chapter also includes all the links to resources that you will require to get going with your own store.

What Is POD?

POD stands for Print on Demand and can be used to get your own art, designs, or brands onto various products. The most common way to utilise POD is through a Shopify app. Shopify is a complete e-commerce platform that you can customise to create your own store. No coding is required and payment methods are taken care of. It is not very cheap with e-commerce stores starting at $29 per month. Other outlets can also to be used such as eBay, Facebook, Etsy, Woo-commerce blogs and your own website.

The POD process works as follows:

- Upload your designs to the POD website or Shopify app.
- Advertise and sell the products with your designs.
- If a customer purchases any of the products the POD Company fulfil the order and ship out to your customer.
- You pocket the difference between your buying price and selling price.

POD Products

The variety of POD products is ever increasing in range with POD companies and end sellers on the rise. Typical products include:

- T-Shirts
- Bags
- Hoodies

- Blankets
- Phone Cases
- Leggings
- Footwear
- Wall Canvasses
- Socks
- Aprons
- And many more…..

POD Companies

Here is a list of POD companies.

- Shine On (https://shineon.com/) - Customised jewellery shipped from the USA.
- Arsadd (http://www.artsadd.com/)
- Printify (https://printify.com/) – Provide a large array of clothing and bags. A very user-friendly Shopify app.
- Printful (https://www.printful.com/) – Also supply a variety clothing and other accessories. They integrate with various platforms such as Etsy.
- Pillow Profits (https://pillowprofits.com/)
- WC Fulfillment (https://wcfulfillment.com/) – Numerous products including phone wallet cases, hooded blankets, and clothing. Their site has some excellent seller resources. Products are shipped from China.
- All Over Print (https://alloverprint.net/) – Hoodies, T-shirts, bags and other accessories. Shipped from the UK.

There are undoubtedly pros and cons to all these suppliers and this is not to provide recommendations but just some research guidance. Some of these POD companies will require you to have a Shopify store. (None of the links are affiliate links).

The POD companies all provide information on how to upload your designs, image size resolution and file types for your designs. Once your design is uploaded the products can be automatically added to your store.

Where to get designs

Designs that sell are often fairly simple so you don't have to spend a fortune obtaining expensive digital artwork. Consider the following options.

Create Your Own

Creating your own designs may be easier than you think. Adobe Photoshop is available for a monthly fee and there are free options such as the online editor Photopea. I created this design with some basic Photoshop skills.

If you are good at art you could look at ways to digitise your work and upload to your POD store or create art using an iPad or Android app. There is also the option of using your own photography.

Hire a Designer

Designers can be found easily on the internet. There are also freelance websites such as Upwork and Fiverr. I have used freelancers on Fiverr for a number of designs including the example below.

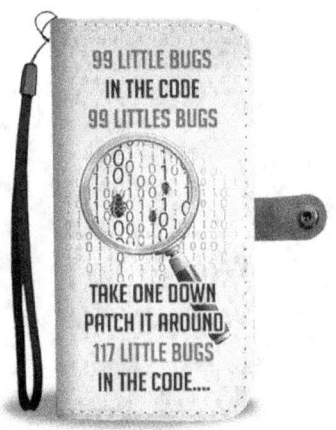

The downside of using these types of sites is that you usually get what you pay for. Look for designers within your budget that have good reviews and offer design revisions.

Stock Images

There are numerous places on the web where you can acquire images and photographs. Some sites you will have to pay a subscription and some will charge for images individually or for a package. There are some free options. I created the design below from a royalty-free image available on the internet.

Here are some free and paid options for you to investigate:

- https://www.shutterstock.com/ – This site requires a subscription or the option of purchasing a bundle of images for a set price.
- https://stock.adobe.com/ – A monthly subscription is required but they offer 1 month free.
- https://pixabay.com/ – Free images.
- https://www.vecteezy.com/ – They offer some free vectors and a premium service that is reasonably priced.
- https://www.freevector.com/ – Free adobe illustrator files can be downloaded. They also offer a premium service.

- https://vectorcharacters.net/ – Free and premium options for cartoon people and animals.
- Google Advanced Image Search – Change the Usage Rights drop-down list at the bottom of the page to 'Free to use, share or modify, even commercially'.
- https://www.stocksy.com/ – Purchase individual royalty free images.

When using images available on the web always ensure that they are free to use for commercial purposes. Also, check that the image resolution is large enough for the product that you will be printing it on, otherwise your design could become pixelated. Image resolution requirements will be available on the POD company's website or app.

Design Ideas

You may have your own designs and brand already in mind. If not I would advise looking at specific niches. Think about your own hobbies and interests. The more specific the niche the better. Think of niches that people are passionate about. For example, rather than targeting people that like dogs, think about dog breeds. Here is a list of niches that I came up with:

- Science teachers
- Computer programmers
- Golfers
- Bird watchers
- Cyclists
- Campers

- Allotment owners or people that have small holdings
- Karate
- Astronomers
- Chefs
- Cheese lovers
- Whiskey lovers
- Armed forces personnel

One of the largest online communities is Reddit. Reddit is a large collection of forums covering a range of topics. Search here for trends and topics. There is a tool called Redditlist which sorts discussion topics based on activity. Reddit can be used to generate ideas for a niche if you search for things like 'what are you passionate about' or 'what makes you happy'. If a community exists here, it will likely exist elsewhere so you can be fairly confident that there will be an audience for your design.

Once you have a niche in mind the next task is to find inspiration for designs. Slogans always do well and you can easily find some inspiration from T-shirt sites and social media. Pinterest is a good place to start and is free. Search for pins related to your niche and look for pins that have been pinned by lots of people. Search on Twitter and Facebook for slogans and images that are trending within your niche.

A research method often used by POD sellers is to check on types of designs that are already selling. Take care not to copy designs, make them your own and use different products. Have a look at some of the spy tools in the list below. Spy tools usually require a monthly fee but remember that from here you will have an idea of types of designs that sell, how many they have sold and more.

- https://teespy.com/
- https://www.teeview.org/

Some other websites to look for inspiration include:

- www.teepublic.com
- www.sunfrog.com
- teespring.com

Shopify Stores

Whilst Shopify store creation is beyond the scope of this article it is important to consider the following points.

Selling Via Other Outlets

If you are new to e-commerce and POD, Shopify is the easiest way to create an online store. However, this service comes at a premium and it can take a lot of work to get your store up to scratch. Consider Etsy or Facebook as a cheaper alternative to get things going if you have no previous experience in creating websites. The downside of this is that you will lose some of the automation provided by using the POD suppliers via their Shopify App. Some suppliers do have Etsy integration so there will not be a problem in these cases. Some suppliers provide Shopify apps only, but this issue can be overcome, see below.

Shopify Plans

Initially, there are only 2 Shopify plans that you need to consider. Shopify Basic and Shopify Lite.

Shopify Basic starts at $29 per month. Included in the package is a full online store with shopping cart and integrated payment systems. A store that looks good and has a professional feel will help to increase sales. This is the best option if you a fairly computer savvy and looking to scale your e-commerce store in the future. There are many online articles and YouTube videos that will help you to create your own Shopify store. Shopify Lite starts at $9 per month. This enables you to use Shopify features but no online store or shopping cart is provided. It is used to integrate your products and payment methods into an already existing website or Facebook business page. So, rather than creating a complete online e-commerce store you could opt to create a Facebook page for your products and integrate Shopify Lite. This will install a 'Shop now' button to your Facebook page and people will be taken to the product gallery when they click it. Products added to Shopify will synchronise to your Facebook store enabling customers to make a purchase without leaving Facebook. Shopify Lite also enables you to install POD suppliers apps. If you were to sell via Etsy using a supplier that does not provide Etsy integration you could use Shopify Lite to process these orders yourself manually through the app. For example, you receive an order through Etsy for a POD product. You would then go to your Shopify dashboard to access the POD company app. From there you would place the order for the product yourself using the customers shipping address obtained from their Etsy order.

Whichever sales outlet you decide to opt for, ensure to go through and check all the settings and options available such as shipping options and your payment details.

Organising Your Store's Products

Before creating your store it is important to consider what products and designs you are going to sell and how you are going to organise them within your store. Shopify enables you to easily categorise your products. So you can group certain products or designs together. Whether using a Shopify website or a Facebook store, a store that is well thought out with products categorised properly will have more appeal than a store with products and designs randomly scattered. A customer expects to see a well-organised store that is easy to navigate. Consider how much effort large online retailers, such as Amazon, put into product categorisation. You may have your own ideas, if not consider the following.

Organise by product – This is the most common way to categorise stores. Using this method you will have separate categories for each product that you sell. The advantage of this is that customers are often familiar with this type of layout and will find it easy to navigate. The downside is that unless you have a solid looking brand with a look and feel that runs through the store it can look a bit messy.

Organise by design – If you have a design within a niche that you are confident will sell, you could categorise your products by design or create a store with just a single design aimed at a particular niche. The advantage of this method is that if a potential customer likes the design and clicks on your advert or link they will be presented with many different products with the same design. This way they may choose to purchase additional items or a different product if they decide that the original product they were browsing is out of their spending range. It also means that you don't have to create loads of designs to get up and running. The downside is that it is more difficult to scale and you will likely need to use a number of POD suppliers.

Single product store with many designs – You may discover a product that will sell and has good profit margins. You could then create a store that specialises in that particular product using various product designs. For example, you could create a store that only sells leggings. The advantage of this method is the simplicity of it as you will only need to deal with a single POD supplier and your target customers will often be similar. The disadvantages are the lack of choice for customers and you will need a number of designs to get your store looking complete.

Please remember that you are not limited to these 3 options. Many online retailers have some very clever intuitive ways to organise their stores. Don't overthink things too much, when starting out you will need to discover products and designs that work. Many beginners create what is referred to as a general store having a mixture of designs, products, and niches (which can still be organised and categorised correctly). Also, note that single products can be added to numerous categories. So, a T-Shirt with a cat design, for example, could be added to a T-Shirt category and a Cat Designs category.

Shopify Themes

If you decide to opt for a Shopify basic plan complete with an online store you will need to consider your Shopify theme. If you have decided not to use Shopify or to use Shopify Lite then this short section will not be relevant.

When you first open the Shopify dashboard and begin creating your website you will need to install a Theme. A Theme is defined by Shopify below.

'A theme is a template that determines the way that your online store looks and feels. Different themes have different styles and layouts, and offer a different experience for your customers. For example, if you're selling spa products, then you probably want your online store to feel relaxed and luxurious. Alternatively, if you're selling electronics, then you might want your online store to look energetic and sleek.'

There are paid and free themes. Free themes are available to install from within your Shopify dashboard. Paid themes will usually be downloaded as a .zip file from a website and then uploaded to your store. Many guides and instructions will often advise you to install a paid theme. This is usually because they have an affiliate link associated with a particular theme and will earn a commission if you use their link and purchase the theme. Paid themes do have their advantages as they often look more unique and are usually more customisable. Most people will opt for a free theme so their stores usually have a similar look and feel. If you are willing to invest the money, then a paid theme is preferable. Have a look at the links below as an example of companies that provides premium themes. There are many other companies and websites available if you conduct a quick google search. Please note that these links are none affiliated links.

https://themeforest.net/category/ecommerce/shopify

https://outofthesandbox.com/

My advice would be to start with a free theme. You can always upgrade your site at a later date to a paid theme if you are having some success. Changing a theme does not affect the content of the website. I would recommend the Debut or Brooklyn themes available from within your Shopify dashboard.

Product Descriptions and Titles

When you upload a design and add products to your store, the product description and title will usually be automatically entered by the POD Company. When it comes to selling online your product title and description is an essential part of landing a sale. I would strongly suggest that you edit them and consider the following.

- Think about your target audience and highlight the aspects of the product that will likely appeal to your audience.
- Highlight the benefits of the product. How can it help the potential customer?
- Use natural language rather than coming across as computer generated.
- Use Power Words! Words such as wondrous, mind-blowing, and stunning. Google search 'sales power words' for more examples.
- Make it easy to scan through. Use bullet points and different size fonts to highlight important information.
- Make sure that you have excellent product images. These can often be obtained from your POD supplier once your designs have been uploaded.
- Be honest, particularly when it comes to production and shipping timescales. If not you will risk complaints further down the line.

Advertising Your Products

Getting your product and brand out there is the most difficult part of this process. Online advertising costs can spiral out of control without even making sales if you are not careful. Having said that, if things are done correctly online advertising can be very effective and can help you make money.

Firstly we shall look at some ways that you can promote your products for little to no cost.

Build a Facebook Group or Instagram Page

If you have the time and patience you could start your own Facebook or Instagram page or group. Once you have enough followers you can start to post your products occasionally. An example of this is a Classic Volkswagen Facebook page that I follow. They post photos of old VW campervans. They have a Facebook store and a link to their Shopify store selling POD products. The page has almost 600,000 likes. Every-time they post a product it is seen by 1000's of people for no additional cost. The advantages of this are that you have plenty of potential customers that have an interest in your niche. The downside is the time and effort to build such a page. You could combine this with paid advertising initially to get the page noticed and gather some followers. Grow your account by been active on a regular basis and check out other accounts or groups for ideas.

Build an Email List

You could build a list of email addresses that you can send product advertisements to. Email lists are often built by offering something that is related to your niche for free. For example, if your products were targeting people that like to bake, you could offer some free recipes in return for their email address. When it then comes to advertising your product you can then email those people. The advantage of this is that you have a ready-made list of potential customers every time you launch a new product or design within your niche. The downside is getting people to see your offer of a free product. You may need to combine this method with some paid advertising initially or build a list alongside a Facebook or Instagram page. It can also take a long time to build a big enough list that can be effective in selling your products. A method of collecting email addresses, such as a website will need to be put in place.

Search Engine Optimisation

If you are web savvy, you could get your website or products ranked highly for particular keywords with online search engines. This can take a long time to achieve and requires a lot of knowledge and research. However, if you manage to get on the first page of Google, for example, you are likely to reach a lot of potential customers. A good place to start is building a blog.

Post to Existing Social Media and Forums

Join related Facebook groups and post links your product or your own Facebook page. Build trust within the group by making a positive contribution or contact the group admin for permission. This method is easy and free but some groups or pages will not tolerate adverts and 'spam'. Consider offering the group admin a small payment or free sample for them to post a link to your product. You could also try Reddit forums even though it's a bit of a long shot you might get lucky and people may share it for you. I would advise against posting directly to related forums and initially try the forum /r/shutupandtakemymoney.

If you are happy to invest in some paid advertising consider the following options.

Instagram Influencers

An Instagram influencer is an Instagram user with a large number of followers, established credibility, and high engagement rates. Influencers may charge anything from $10's to $1000's. The only way to find out if they are willing to promote your product and how much they will charge is to contact them. If they have an email address within their bio send them an email with your proposal to check that they are willing to work with you. Ensure that they have a minimum of 100k followers and that each picture has a few thousand likes. Initially try to use influencers that charge between $10 and $30. You could also follow similar principles for Twitter.

Google and Bing Ads

Search engine ads place links to your website on their search results page based on keywords, search queries, and other factors. The advantage of this method is that people have conducted a search for your type of product, so if they click on your link there is a good chance of landing a sale. Having said that, I personally believe that most POD products are more likely to be purchased on impulse.

Facebook Ads

When it comes to using paid advertising for POD this is my preferred method. It enables you to target your ads to specific people that are likely to be interested in your niche. Facebook advertising can be very complex, expensive, and difficult to understand. My advice is to keep it simple to start with, set a budget, and test your ads, designs, and audiences.

There is also the option of using paid advertising within Etsy, Amazon, and eBay. If you do decide to utilise paid adverting I would advise learning about your preferred method first. If not, you could end up wasting money. Look for beginners help and courses online. There is a lot of free and cheap information out there on outlets such as YouTube or Udemy. Start with the social media platform that you are most familiar with as an end user. Some of the POD suppliers provide guidance on advertising. WC Fulfillment offers a free Facebook advertising mini course.

Start-up Cost Summary

Costs can vary and this all depends on your budget and skills. These costs are in line with how I started which involved building my own Shopify store with a free theme.

- Shopify – $29 per calendar month
- Designs – Initially I struck a deal for 10 designs for $100 from Fiverr. I also created some of my own to get my store looking busy and active.
- Facebook Advertising – I spent an initial $200 on testing designs and audiences for my niche. Advertising is still an ongoing cost. However much you spend, it needs to be constantly monitored to ensure that you are achieving a return on your investment.

The Pros

- As we have seen, it can be a relatively cheap way to start your own business. You can start as small or as large as you feel comfortable.
- You can create your own brand and USP rather than competing with others to sell the exact same products online.
- There is no need to invest in inventory.
- Fulfillment is taken care of. There is no packing and delivery for you to carry out.
- Upon store completion it can become almost 100% automated, leaving you time to concentrate on advertising and promoting your products.

- There is potential to create a scalable business that is relatively easy to grow and expand.
- You can sell to audiences within a niche that you know and like.

The Cons

- Competition is growing and many niches are saturated.
- Profit margins are usually fairly small.
- Additional fees such as Paypal, Etsy and Amazon seller fees need to be considered. Bank charges may also apply depending on your currency and location.
- Production and shipping times mean that some products can take up to 4 weeks to reach the customer.
- The cost of advertising is ever increasing.

Plan of Attack!

If you have no clue where to start, follow the steps below.

1. Research a niche – Generate a list of 10 potential niches and research them to see if there is likely to be an audience. Begin to narrow it down by excluding niches that you think are likely to be too saturated or not wide enough.
2. Research Designs – Used the methods described to generate some design ideas. Save the images

or screenshots so that you can share them with your designer

3. Plan your store – Make notes on how you would like to set your store up. Think of a store name and look into the POD suppliers to decide which products you would like to sell.

4. Create Designs – Either outsource or create your own designs.

5. Create your store – Build your store and outsource anything that you cannot do by yourself.

6. Install POD apps – Install the apps if you are using Shopify and upload your designs.

7. Social Media – Create your social media accounts and link them to your store. Create some content, make them look busy and active.

8. Begin advertising and start selling!

Summary

Despite the drawbacks, making a profit from your own e-commerce store is hugely rewarding. My store ticks away in the background with just a few hours work and attention dedicated weekly. I ensure that my ads are performing and occasionally add some more designs. Like any business, it all comes down to the time and money that you are willing to invest. Some POD store owners spend $1000's monthly on advertising and make a lot of money. Whereas others, like myself, are happy to enjoy the additional income without the huge risks.

If you do decide to create your own POD store, I wish you luck and I hope that you have found this information useful.

How to Make Money Affiliate Marketing with Clickbank

In this chapter, we shall be covering everything you need to know to make money online as an affiliate marketer through Clickbank. Here we provide you with all the resources required in order to get started creating a passive income.

We shall be going through where you can sign up as an affiliate marketer; the types of products that you should select for promotion and what to avoid; where and how to promote and advertise your selected products using paid and free methods; the costs to get started; the pros and cons of this method; a 'plan of attack'; and a list of trusted affiliate marketing programs.

Affiliate marketing involves recommending a company's products or services to potential customers, generating a sale and earning a commission in return.

We shall be focusing on Clickbank's affiliate program. Clickbank has a free and easy sign-up process that doesn't request additional stipulations when you sign up, such as your own website or a high traffic social media page. Once you become more experienced at making money online you may progress into other avenues such as the Amazon affiliate program. You will be able to use many of the strategies described in this article to promote products from other affiliate programs.

What is Clickbank and how does it Work?

Clickbank provides an outlet for vendors to sell their products over the internet. They offer secure payment and fraud protection. They also offer a return and refund policy to the end customers.

People can sign up as an affiliate and promote the products to earn a commission on the sales. Affiliates use a 'Hoplink' (provided by Clickbank) that directs the customer to the vendor's website. If a customer clicks the Hoplink and makes a purchase the affiliate receives a percentage commission.

You can sign up as an affiliate here: https://www.clickbank.com/affiliate-network/

Selecting the Right Products

There are hundreds of products available for promotion including physical products, digital products, courses, memberships, books, and many more items.

One of the advantages of Clickbank is the ability to see how well, or not so well, products are selling. The aim is to find items that have a selling record so that we know people will buy it. However, we want to avoid products that are selling a lot as the competition will be too high. It is also useful to know how much we can expect to earn from a sale. Clickbank provides some stats so that we can easily find this information.

Once you have signed up to Clickbank, click the 'Marketplace' link at the top of the page. Now, on the left of the page, the product categories will be displayed. Select a category of your choice to list the products within it.

For each product we have the following information: The title and link to the vendor's product page; a brief description of the product; a link to the affiliate support page if they have one and a vendor contact email address; a 'Promote' button used to generate your Hoplink; and the option to add the product to a list of favourites.

Below this, we have a list of Stats.

- Initial $/sale: This is the dollar value paid on average for the initial sale only.
- Avg %/sale: This is the percentage of the total sale that the affiliate receives from the initial sale and

additional sales such as upsells or recurring payments.

- Avg Rebill Total: This is the average amount received for rebill amounts only, such as upsells or recurring payments.
- Avg %/rebill: This is the average percentage received for rebill amounts only, such as upsells or recurring payments.
- Grav: Short for gravity, this is the stat that helps us determine how well the product is selling. It is an approximate performance stat that gives an indication of how many affiliates have successfully sold the product. Generally speaking, the higher the number the more sales have been made.

Consider the following points when looking for Clickbank products to promote.

- Try to find for products that you have an interest in, have some existing knowledge on, or you can easily research. This will help with promoting the product further down the line.
- Try to find products that have an affiliate support page. This will also assist you in promoting the product in the future.
- Do not select products based solely on the amount you can earn. Remember that higher cost products will be more difficult to convert into sales.
- Products that can solve an urgent problem are preferable as they are more likely to lead to sales.
- Check their landing page. Would it make you want to buy if you had a need for that product? Look at it from the customer's point of view, not just your own.

- Look at the product's gravity. Aim for a gravity rating of between 1 and 60 (inclusive) with the optimum between 10 and 20.

The aim of these pointers is to get you up and running. As you learn more about what works for yourself and effective ways to promote items, you will begin to build your own systems and ways of working.

Promoting Your Selected Products

To generate sales we need to drive traffic to the vendor's sale page. There are a number of free and paid methods that we can use to achieve this. Before we look at ways we can promote the products it is important to understand some simple internet marketing terms.

Direct Linking – the potential customer clicks on your ad and is sent directly to the vendor's offer page.

Landing or Squeeze Page – a web page which serves as the entry point for the vendor's offer page. You could create a landing page that offers something free or further information in return for an email address. The potential customer is then directed to the vendor's offer page via the Hoplink.

The advantages of having a landing page are that you can build a list of email addresses of people that you know have an interest in that type of product. You can then use this list to advertise directly in the future. You can also build trust by maintaining contact with the customer as not everyone will make a purchase straight away. Landing pages are known statistically to increase conversions.

If you do not wish to make your own website and would like to create a landing page that collects email addresses and has an automatic email autoresponder have a look at https://www.getresponse.com/. You could consider outsourcing a landing page on Fiverr or creating a free WordPress page. Adobe has a free one-page website builder called Adobe Spark.

Research other landing pages advertising similar products and investigate what they offer and how they entice people into clicking their link or providing an email address. Landing pages will usually include:

1. A headline or a hook to tempt people to continue reading.
2. A bulleted list of benefits or solutions to a problem.
3. A call to action such as email input form in return for something (coupon codes, information, discounts, and so on).

All of this information should be available on the vendor's affiliate page.

Inbound Advertising/Marketing – When a potential customer searches for a solution to a problem. They may, for example, go to an online search engine to find products that can help them. The customer is seeking a product.

Outbound Advertising/Marketing – The vendor or marketer is seeking customers.

Pay-Per-Click Advertising

We can use search engines such as Google, Yahoo, and Bing to 'buy' visits to the Vendor's website (direct linking) or our own landing page. Each time the ad is clicked they charge a fee.

If you decide to use PPC advertising, I would advise starting with Bing. They have a cheaper cost per link click when compared to Google. Bing is also more affiliate friendly. Google will often prevent marketers from running ads containing an affiliate link. Prior to signing up, search for Bing Ad promotions. They often have deals offering credit, in which case you can learn, practice and trial this system for free.

I would recommend further research on creating PPC ads. There are a lot of settings and mistakes can be costly. You can, however, follow the general process and guidelines below for creating PPC ads with Bing once you have registered:

1. Click to 'Create a new campaign' and set the goal of the campaign to 'Visit my website'.

2. Name the campaign and set the daily budget. I would suggest no more than $5 during your learning phase of this advertising method.
3. Click the daily budget options and set to 'Accelerated' to get as many clicks as possible.
4. Opt to select specific locations and choose countries that use the same languages as the vendor's website offers. Always include the USA as this is a known high converting area for this type of marketing. Remove the option to include 'People searching for or viewing pages about the targeted location'.
5. Save and move onto the next page.
6. Enter the web address of the target. This is the vendor's product page, not your affiliate link.
7. Here you can enter your search keywords. We shall discuss how to generate keywords later in the post.
8. Click next page to create the ad.
9. In the 'Final URL' text box enter the URL of the vendor's selling page again.
10. Enter the title, subheading, and text for your ad. Check other ads for inspiration or check the affiliate page from the vendor which may include examples that you can use.
11. Click save and next step.
12. Set the bid strategy to manual so that you can target your own list of keywords.
13. As a guide, set the 'Ad group bid' to 1% of the amount that you are set to make from the sale. For example, if your commission is $15 set this to $0.15. Save the ad.

14. In the left-hand pane select your new campaign by its name. Select the Ads tab and scroll down to select the edit icon for the ad.
15. Click 'Ad URL Options' and paste your affiliate link obtained from Clickbank into the 'Tracking Template' text box.
16. Click save and run the ad when you are ready.

Keywords are the most important factor when creating PPC ads. The aim is to create plenty of keywords related to the product that you are selling. Avoid using only the suggestions made by Bing when creating your ad. The websites below can help to create a list of keywords.

Uber Suggest – https://neilpatel.com/ubersuggest/

Moz Keyword explorer – https://moz.com/explorer

There are 3 main types of keywords.

Broad – The search does not have to match your keyword exactly. Things like spelling mistakes would not be an issue for a broad match keyword.

Exact – This means that the search must match your keywords exactly in order for your ad to be considered for listing.

Phrase – This aims to be somewhere between the other 2 keyword types. It doesn't have to be exact but they are usually more targeted than broad keywords.

Include all three types of keywords in your ad by using the website – https://www.keywordmatchtypetool.com/

After 5-7 days remove any keywords or alter keyword bids for keywords that are not performing or that are too expensive. It is also advisable to try different ads. Check the ad CTR (Click Through Rate) every 5-7 days and cancel the worst performing ads. Experiment with different ads and keyword lists utilising your free Bing ads introductory credit. Avoid editing existing ads as this can affect the ad performance. Instead, copy the ad, make the necessary alterations, set the new ad running and deactivate the original ad. Abandon ads, or the product, if you have spent double the commission value without making a sale.

The downside of this type of advertising is the cost. Paying for clicks does not guarantee sales and advertising can become expensive. You should expect an initial loss.

However, if you find an ad that works the return on investment will pay off. This is a fast, targeted approach that uses the preferred inbound marketing method. The alternative or additional, way to generate traffic from search engines is to use search engine optimisation (SEO). SEO would need a website and lots of time before we would yield any reward.

Facebook Review Pages

Before a customer commits to making a purchase online they will often search for an independent product review. The aim of this marketing technique is to create a Facebook product review page that is on the first page of google for the search term '[product name] review'.

This method can be used with direct linking and a landing page. You will need to include your link on the page description and in your posts. Facebook does not always permit affiliate links. Use https://bitly.com/ to alter your link and test that Facebook permits the link before building your page.

If you are familiar with Facebook this is a very simple but effective process. Consider the following points when creating your Facebook product review page:

- Name the page '[product name] review'.
- Contact friends and ask them to 'like' the page to create more trust when people visit the page.
- Ensure that there is no existing Facebook product review page.
- Create regular posts, at least weekly. Check the resources available from the vendor's affiliate page including testimonials and reviews. Share useful articles from the web or re-write your own content.
- Consider spending a small amount (less than $20) on Facebook advertising to increase page 'likes' and therefore search engine rankings. 'Likes' can be purchased from places like India where the cost to advertise on Facebook is considerably cheaper.

Even when utilising the power of Facebook it can take time to reach the first page of google. With an active page it will take a minimum of 2 – 3 months and even then it is still a gamble. Sales are not guaranteed.

However, if your page is regularly attracting visitors you will likely achieve sales and for very little investment you could generate a steady passive income stream.

YouTube Product Reviews

This is a similar method to creating a Facebook product review page, except the aim is to generate traffic via a review video uploaded to YouTube. This method can also be used with direct linking or a landing page. Include links in your video and in the video description. Use https://bitly.com/ if required.

View other review videos for inspiration. You will also need to obtain the product. Contact the vendor, explain what your aim is and try to negotiate a discount or a trial. If the product is digital use https://www.ezvid.com/download to record your screen activity (screencasting).

This technique is more suited to Amazon affiliate marketing but can also be effective with certain products in Clickbank if done correctly. It can be used in conjunction with other promotional avenues. The video could be embedded on a landing page, a Facebook page or the video link posted to other places as we shall discover in the following section.

Commenting and Posting Outlets

There are numerous places where we can post comments and links to help drive traffic to the vendor's selling page via a Hoplink. For this to be successful you will need to become an active and productive member of these groups. Provide value and useful information for other group members. An informative landing page, blog, Facebook review page, YouTube video, or combination is preferable. People will not take kindly to direct linked adverts. But, if you bide your time and can offer something helpful to other members, this technique can be very effective.

Try different techniques when it comes to posting or commenting. A softer approach is to pose a question such as, 'Hi, do you guys think this is any good? [link to landing page]'.

This technique is not necessarily aiming to immediately direct the people that you are conversing with. The main purpose is to have your link viewed and clicked by people that have conducted an online search on a particular topic and are reading the posts and comments for answers to a problem. The advantage of this is that your comment containing your link can remain there, hopefully generating sales. Once you are aware of this method you will begin to notice other people adopting similar techniques.

Forums

Whatever product you decide to promote, there will almost certainly be online forums related to it. Use a search engine to find forums, join them and start posting!

In addition to this, there are general forums such as Reddit that will contain categories or subcategories related to your selected product's niche.

Facebook Groups

Very similar to forums are Facebook groups. Again, join them and provide group members with some value.

Blog Comment Section

Most blogs have a comment section underneath the main article. Find blogs and articles related to the product that you are promoting.

Quora

Quora can often be found near the top end of search engines rankings when you search for information on a particular topic.

The Pros

- It is a quick relatively simple way to make a passive income.
- It is an inexpensive way to make money online.
- It can be made sustainable by collecting email addresses using a landing page.
- No initial investment in physical products or in creating your own product is required.
- It is an excellent way to learn and practice affiliate marketing.

The Cons

- Direct linking is not a sustainable income method.
- Some products on Clickbank appear 'scammy'.

- It's a bit of a gamble. However much effort you put in, you are not guaranteed to make an income.
- Customer returns are relatively high with Clickbank. If a customer returns a product, within a given timescale, you lose the commission.

Plan of Attack

If you are not sure where to begin and would like to get started with minimal investment, follow the process below:

1. Register and enter your details with Clickbank.
2. Select a product based on the criteria set out earlier.
3. Join forums and groups related to your selected product and gradually build up your activity. Post or comment 2 – 5 times per week.
4. Search for a Bing ads promotion and register.
5. Start and end your ads based on the criteria set out earlier using direct linking to the vendor's selling page. Experiment with 1 product initially.
6. Create either a free WordPress landing page or a Facebook product review page. Ensure that you include useful content and your Hoplink.
7. Begin posting your landing page link or Facebook review page to all of the outlets described earlier.
8. Repeat for different products, emitting paid advertising if you wish.

Summary

Affiliate marketers must be patient. It takes time to discover methods that work for yourself and particular products. If you decide to invest in advertising or creating landing pages, I would advise further reading on internet marketing to ensure that your ads and sales copy are as effective as possible.

However, once your links are out there who knows what could happen?! You could generate sales and income for years to come with little to no financial investment.

Also remember that this is an introduction to affiliate marketing designed to provide you with quick, cheap, and effective methods to achieve a return. Consider these other affiliate programs:

- Amazon Associates
- eBay Partners
- Rakuten
- Shopify
- Share a Sale
- Awin
- Target Affiliates
- Click Funnels
- FriendFinder
- Market Health
- eHarmony
- Betfair

In addition to the methods already covered, other ways to promote products or services include:

- Creating a blog or website on a particular product niche or subject.

- Create a social media presence using Facebook or Instagram.
- Write an e-book on the best way to use their service (dating or gambling).
- Create videos, such as how to make a Shopify store for example.
- Offer promos, coupons, incentives or loyalty rewards.
- Offer something free or cheap on the premise that they sign up for a service.
- Create an e-commerce store that receives commission payments without having to source, stock, and ship products.

Make Money Online Offering Free Websites

In this chapter, we shall go through how to generate an online income using a unique affiliate marketing system and how almost anyone can create websites and make money from them.

We shall cover: what affiliate marketing is; how to create websites yourself or how to outsource the work; where to get content and images for websites; where to find customers and how to approach them; what and how you can upsell additional services to make more money from a single sale; the costs of starting up; the pros and cons of this type of business; and a 'plan of attack' for getting started.

The Aim

The process of how we can make money online using this method is as follows:

1. Offer small business owners their own website for a small fee or even for free.
2. Direct them to a web hosting company using your affiliate link (all websites must have hosting). You will receive a lump sum commission.
3. Once they have signed up, they provide you with their login information.
4. Install WordPress for them and create the pages as promised or outsource the work.
5. Upsell other services.

Affiliate Marketing with Hostgator

Affiliate marketing involves recommending a company's products or services to potential customers, generating a sale and earning a commission in return.

The service that we shall use for this particular example is Hostgator website hosting. Anyone can sign up to the https://www.hostgator.com/affiliates. There are numerous other companies providing very similar programs, simply Google 'web hosting affiliate programs' and take your pick.

I used Hostgator as it is reasonably well known and they offer a good program. The information below is taken from their website and shows what you can earn depending on the number of signups per month.

- 1-5   **$50** per signup
- 6-10   **$75** per signup
- 11-20 **$100** per signup
- 21+   **$125** per signup

Create Your Demo Website

In order to demonstrate to your customers what they can expect to receive, you will first need to create your own website. This also enables you to practice going through the process ready for when you receive your first order.

If you do not wish to create your own demo website you can still use your affiliate links in any way you wish. Send them in emails, messenger services, or via a social media page.

There are 2 options for creating websites. Either learn the process of creating a basic WordPress website yourself (if you do not already know) or outsource online via Fiverr. If you decide to outsource the work, I would recommend using Fiverr for this method as it is likely to be the cheapest option.

WordPress websites are very easy to make and there are countless videos guides available on YouTube. Watch some tutorials on 'creating a wordpress website with hostgator' to determine if you think that creating your own Website is achievable. Notice that YouTubers' will also have an affiliate link within their video descriptions.

Here is a link to my Website. Feel free to use the wording and if you are feeling generous you can use my affiliate link when signing up to Hostgator.

www.small-business-websites.uk

If you decide to outsource the work, search on Fiverr for 'WordPress websites' or 'basic wordpress websites' and consider the following:

- You may need to charge your customers in order to cover the cost of outsourcing the work. For example, offer websites for $50 rather than for free. Ensure that you receive payment upfront, so as not to lose out.
- Do not always choose the cheapest freelancer. Check what they are offering. Have a look at their package to ensure it includes what you require such as the number of web pages and content upload.
- Aim to pay no more than $50.
- Offer your customers the exact same as what the freelancer on Fiverr is offering.
- Examine the option of completing some of the work yourself in order to keep costs down. You could, for example, upload the text content. Or you could do the bulk of the work yourself and outsource things like logo or header designs.
- After a bit of searching, I found this freelancer who appears to fit the bill – https://www.fiverr.com/webpressguru

If possible, I recommend creating the websites yourself because: it keeps the costs and therefore risks to a minimum; it provides you with a new skill that you can utilise and develop; it enables you to be more flexible in the services that you are able offer; and it also enables you to easily up-sell other services (more on this later).

Website Content and Images

Your customer may wish to provide you with their own content and images. If not, then you can either offer it as an extra or include it in your price. To make life easier for yourself download some generic images related to various industries or businesses that you are likely to be targeting. Have them ready and organised so that you can quickly access them when it comes to creating a website.

Here are some free and paid options for website images:

- https://www.shutterstock.com/ – This site requires a subscription or the option of purchasing a bundle of images for a set price.
- https://stock.adobe.com/ – A monthly subscription is required but they offer 1 month free.
- https://pixabay.com/ – Free images.
- https://www.vecteezy.com/ – They offer some free vectors and a premium service that is reasonably priced.
- https://www.freevector.com/ – Free adobe illustrator files can be downloaded. They also offer a premium service.
- https://vectorcharacters.net/ – Free and premium options for cartoon people and animals.
- Google Advanced Image Search – Change the Usage Rights drop-down list at the bottom of the

page to 'Free to use, share or modify, even commercially'.

- https://www.stocksy.com/ — Purchase individual royalty free images.

Creating written content is a bit trickier and very time-consuming. Have a look at other websites for inspiration and have some relevant content ready to copy and paste into the websites. This can always be easily edited at a later date. For the majority of clients, I would initially enter a fairly generic introductory text content. The client could email or message if they require any revisions. I also email them a simple guide so that they can edit it themselves although this often proved to be more trouble than it was worth and I ended up editing it for them anyway!

Finding Customers and Advertising Your Services

Firstly it is important to think about your potential customers. I believe that the type of people that may require this type of service are small business owners that do not have the time or knowledge to develop their online presence. You may have some other ideas, but if not, a quick easy way to generate ideas is to look at the competition. Investigate their target customers and any potential gaps in the market.

Think about small start-ups and sole traders such as tilers, plumbers, mobile hairdressers, beauty therapists, photographers, independent store owners, roofers, driving instructors, mobile cleaners, and mechanics. The list is very extensive.

The tricky part is finding and approaching your potential customers. As you are targeting people that are not very internet savvy, I do believe that traditional marketing methods such as mail drops and advertising in local publications would be effective. However, the method that I decided to adopt was to contact people that were trying to increase their own customer base on the Facebook market place and Facebook local selling groups. The advantages of this are that it is free, you can do it from the comfort of your front room on your computer or smartphone, and you can target anywhere in the world (within reason). The downside is that you need to contact a lot of people. I would estimate that for every 100 people that I contacted, between 2 and 6 people responded.

The process I follow is:

1. I created my own Facebook page for my service showcasing my offers.
2. I joined different sales and advertising groups all over the country (using my personal account). I did this by searching on Facebook for groups within towns, villages, and cities. For example, I would search in Facebook groups for 'For sale Leeds' or 'sale and swap Plymouth'. These groups often contain 1000's of people.
3. I then look through the ads and identify any posted by sole traders and small business owners.
4. I then comment on their post or message them directly if I am feeling brave! Have your text ready

so that you can simply copy and paste your message rather than typing it out each time.

I send them a script similar to this:

Hi Joe, we can help you increase custom with your own website for just £10 as we are looking to build our portfolio. The offer is limited to a few locally based businesses. Feel free to inbox me if this is something that you will benefit from.

If people respond I ask them for a phone number or an email address so that I could provide them with further information. You could even email them the basic steps to get started including your affiliate link. Be honest and explain that there will be a small hosting fee that every website owner in the world is subject to.

I also found that charging a small initial fee, as opposed to offering sites for free, is more effective. This is because it means that people have made a small commitment and are more likely to sign up to Hostgator. I take these payments via Paypal or a bank transfer.

Upselling

Once you have landed a customer that has signed up via your affiliate link, you are in a great position to begin offering other services. You could offer them monthly or weekly edits for a fixed fee where you add posts, information or images for them. You could offer graphics or logo designs that you can then outsource to a freelancer. You could also offer additional website features such as a map showing their location or a customer contact form. These types of features are all available for free within WordPress using plugins. You could also charge to create their content for them if you wish.

A fantastic upsell is the offer of search engine optimisation with the aim of being listed high in the google rankings for a particular keyword or search phrase. This may be easier than you think. I have managed to get a number of websites on the first page of Google by following this process:

1. Register the site domain with Google and follow their instructions for proving the site ownership/administration access. You will need a Gmail account to do this.
2. Wait for confirmation from Google and check that your site is registered with them by conducting a google search for the site URL. If the site is listed then the registration has been successful.
3. Access the site's Wordpress admin dashboard and install the plugin 'Yoast SEO'.
4. Use the SEO plugin to target a keyword or phrase. Follow the criteria set out by the plugin and create your website text content.

The key to achieving success using this method is targeting a phrase that will only apply locally. In the following example, I created a website for someone that was selling mattresses in the Huddersfield area in the North of England. We agreed to target the search term 'Mattresses Huddersfield'. This website is currently on the first page of Google for this search term. If you conduct the search you will see it – www.bedfactoryonline.co.uk.

Now, if I had decided to target just the word 'Mattresses', I would not likely have achieved the same success. This is because huge companies are competing for that keyword across the country or even world. They invest huge amounts of money into their SEO and I would have struggled to compete. The mattress seller only wanted local sales anyway, so this method worked perfectly for him.

With upsells, I managed to make over £300 from this sale (commission, SEO and extra features), from what was originally just a £10 website. He continues to achieve sales through this website.

When it came to charging for SEO I offered it as risk-free, meaning that he did not have to pay me unless the website reached the first page of Google for the key phrase that we had agreed. Upon completion, he was to pay me £200, which is really rather cheap for SEO. If he hadn't completed his side of the deal, I would have simply de-registered the site with Google. Note that SEO can take time. It may be weeks or months until you see results. Make your customer aware of this, keep checking on things, and be patient. You could even follow this process for your own website targeting your local area initially.

Another avenue for upselling is social media management. You could create their social media pages for them and generate some content. Increase their pages engagement by running competitions or advertisements.

Startup Costs

Starting your own business or side-line does not come much cheaper than this. What you spend depends largely on yourself and how much of the work you are willing to complete. For me personally, the only cost is approximately £3 per month for the hosting of my website. I have outsourced some of the work such as logo designs and website header designs, but these costs were passed onto the customers.

What it has cost me is my time. When I first began, it took me many hours to complete a WordPress website before it was at a standard that I and the customer were happy with. It really did not seem to be worth the effort. Now I can get a reasonable website up and running in less than a couple of hours, so the return feels more rewarding.

The Pros

- It is a really cheap way to start a side business.
- You can provide unbeatable value.
- After some initial learning and with a system in place, you can quickly and easily create numerous websites.
- It can be run entirely over the internet and you can target any location.
- You will develop a really useful skill, creating websites.
- There are huge numbers of potential customers that would like a website but are concerned about costs.

- The commission payments are good compared to other affiliate programs.

The Cons

- The return on time investment is poor in the initial stages.
- It can be difficult and disheartening when trying to drum up business.
- A degree of sales is involved which does not come naturally to a lot of people including myself.
- Customers may let you down. They have the option to cancel their Hostgator subscription within a given number of days. If they do this, the time and money that you have invested will be lost.
- Learning how to make a website can be time-consuming and frustrating at times.

Plan of Attack

If you have no clue where to start, follow the steps below.

1. Do your research. Look at web design company websites, gather ideas, speak to family and friends, decide if you would like to outsource or not, and create a list of freelancers on Fiverr that could help you.

2. Gather collections of royalty free images and organise them into folders related to industries or business that you are likely to target.
3. Create some generic written content that you can quickly copy and paste into the websites.
4. Go to Hostgator and follow the process to create your own website.
5. Offer family or friends a free website and a share of the commission if you wish. Thus gaining additional practice and experience.
6. Create your social media accounts and link them to your website. Create some content, make them look busy and active.
7. Join the Facebook marketplace and sales groups.
8. Begin approaching potential customers.

Summary

This is a great method to generate some extra income whilst providing you with the opportunity to learn and develop some really useful skills for making money online.

I have tended to use this method as something that I come back to every few months when I need a bit of a financial boost. If I were to do it constantly it would feel like I was pestering too many people on the sales groups. Having said that, there are many other sales and marketing strategies that you could use to really push on with this side business.

I hope that you have found this information useful and I would like to wish you luck in starting your own web design business!

Make Money Online with Your Own team of Freelancers

In this chapter, we shall cover how anyone can generate an online income finding and outsourcing digital freelance work.

We shall be looking at: the aims and objectives of this money making method; where to source deals; the type of deals to look for and how to land them; where to outsource deals and create a team; the pros and cons of this method; and a plan of attack.

In summary, we are looking for clients that require digital work or a digital product to be created for them using an outsourcing website. It could be anything from logo design to building an entire website. The aim is to offer to do the work for them, outsource to someone that can do the work cheaper, and pocket the difference.

Whilst on the face of it this may seem dishonest, the client is achieving their goal of getting the work done to an agreed standard at an agreed price. You are taking away much of the hassle associated with outsourcing work such as finding good quality designers or marketers. Additionally, many cheaper freelancers are non-native English speakers. Working with them and communicating can be challenging at times and many clients do not want any added difficulties. For the freelancer, you are providing them with additional work and the potential to work with you on numerous projects in the future for a price that they have decided is fair.

In the longer term, the aim is to project manage larger tasks using a select number of freelancers that you have regular contact with. Thus creating your own team that you can work with efficiently.

Finding Freelance Jobs

Upwork.com is a great place to source suitable freelance jobs. Here 1000's of jobs are posted daily, usually by clients that are willing to spend more on their digital requirements when compared to clients of other freelance websites. Upwork also holds the client payment until you have fulfilled the requested work ensuring that you will get paid upon completion. Another advantage of using Upwork is that they have a relatively high limit on how many jobs you can bid for from a free account. The downside to using Upwork is the difficulty in getting jobs when you have no previous work record. We shall cover how to overcome this issue later.

Creating an Upwork Account

Upon creating your Upwork profile, aside from regular account details, you will be asked for information such as your skill sets. The aim at this stage is to successfully create an account that is not rejected by Upwork, you can edit your profile and details at a later date. To avoid your application being rejected ensure to enter skill sets that target specific niches. Avoid really common skills such as logo design.

In your title and overview enter some information that ties in with the skill sets that you listed. This is, along with your list of skill sets, the most significant section for ensuring that your application is accepted. Make it readable and inform clients that samples of work can be provided upon request. Enter some education and employment details if you wish to help get the profile accepted.

When setting your hourly rate, enter what you would consider being a reasonable rate, $20 – $30 should be fine. We shall be focusing on set price jobs so this is not something that we need to be too concerned about.

Clients are more likely to select you for a job based on your submitted sales proposal, rather than your profile (more on this later). However, it is a good idea to return to your profile and modify it as you complete more jobs.

It is very common for applications to be rejected, don't quit at the first hurdle. This is usually due to the skills that have been selected and too many freelancers within Upwork already offering those skills. Selecting certain skills does not mean that we can only apply for jobs related to those skills, we can update the skill sets at a later date. To ensure that the application is accepted, we can follow the process below to find skills that are more specific.

1. Go to www.upwork.com/find-work
2. Select a category of your choice to view some of the jobs.
3. Beneath each job description will be a list of skills pertaining to that job.
4. Click on a skill and a new page will open showing all the jobs relevant to that skill and the total number of jobs found at the top of the page.
5. Find skills that have less than 150 jobs associated with them.
6. Add these skills to your profile and remove any skills that have too many jobs. Aim for less than 5 really specific niche skills.
7. Re-submit your application.

Finding Freelancers

Fiverr.com is one of the most economical ways to complete digital jobs using a freelancer. It is an easy website to join, freelancers are clearly categorised, it has a rating system, and you can check work portfolios.

Selecting Jobs and Making Proposals

Once you have been approved conduct a job search, within Upwork, applying the filter 'Fixed Price'. Narrow down the number of jobs by focusing on specific niche skills. Browse for jobs that include plenty of details specifying their requirements in the description. Check the client's history and reviews to ensure they are serious. Make a note of the price that they are willing to pay.

Assuming that this is your first time going through this process, you now need to go to Fiverr to find a suitable freelancer to complete the work. Conduct a search and view some of the relevant freelancer profiles. Check their reviews, portfolio, and their prices ensuring that you can make a profit. Take into consideration the Upwork percentage fee.

As you will likely have no previous work experience or reviews on Upwork, you will need to contact the freelancer to obtain examples or work demos. Offer transparency and explain to them that you are aiming to put together a small team of freelancers for a selected client. Explain that there will be numerous projects moving forward and go on to request permission to show the client examples of your work. Most people will be more than happy to co-operate. If they are not, try someone else. If you have an idea of the jobs types that you wish to apply for, you may wish to save a selection of freelancers and their work examples prior to searching for jobs on Upwork.

Once you have found a suitable freelancer on Fiverr, you need to go back to Upwork and submit a proposal for the selected job. Ensure your listed skill sets match the job. When it comes to writing the cover letter there are 3 important factors to include:

1. Make it more personal by using the client's name or username and write a different proposal for every client. Most freelancers will simply copy and paste the same information each time. Avoiding this tactic will help you stand out.
2. Show that you understand their requirements – eg 'I have seen from your listed job that you require *xyz*'.
3. Show them proof that you can do it. Attach work examples or demos provided by your freelancer on Fiverr.

If you wish, you can provide transparency by informing the client that you have a team that will be able to assist them. You can also create an agency account in Upwork.

Competition is fierce. Do not give up after submitting 1 or 2 job proposals. Winning your first gig is the most difficult. You will need to submit numerous proposals in the initial stages, but it will become easier.

Once your job is accepted and funded in Upwork, go ahead and purchase the gig on Fiverr.

Other Potential Client Arenas

In addition to Upwork, there are forums and Facebook groups that you could consider for jobs:

- Facebook groups for print on demand sellers that require product designs.
- Groups for writers and self-publishers that require proofreading, formatting and cover designs.
- Web designers that require assistance.
- Computer programmers.
- And many more......

As an example, upon creating my print on demand store I posted in a Facebook group requesting information for recommended designers. I was contacted by a group member who informed me she had a team of designers that could complete the work as requested. I was aware that she was simply outsourcing the work, most likely on Fiverr. However, I was more than happy to proceed as it saved me the hassle of finding suitable freelancers for my designs and left me with more time to concentrate on building my store. This is what gave me the idea for this method.

The Pros

- There are little to no start-up costs if you have a web-enabled device and an internet connection. Both Fiverr and Upwork have an app.
- You can start making money online in a short timescale.
- This is a scalable model. You can grow your freelance team and your Upwork reputation.

The Cons

- It can be tricky creating an Upwork account.
- There is a lot of competition on Upwork and landing jobs can be difficult.
- Upwork limit the number of jobs that you can make a proposal for.
- There is a small risk of losing out. If the client decides to dispute the work you have provided you could lose the amount that was paid to the freelancer on Fiverr.

Plan of Attack!

Follow this action plan to get started.

1. Register on Upwork.
2. Register on Fiverr.
3. Search for suitable jobs on Upwork. Start with smaller jobs, to begin with, building up credibility and confidence.
4. Search for suitable freelancers on Fiverr, request examples and demos.
5. Submit your job proposals on Upwork.

Summary

This is a really simple but effective way of making money online. Like anything, there will be hurdles as you are having to manage people and deal with clients. Use the Upwork and Fiverr apps so that you can respond quickly.

It can be difficult in the early stages, but as you build up a work history on Upwork and gather a regular reliable team on Fiverr it starts to run a lot smoother. Once you have a set team, that you know and trust, you could opt to deal with them outside of Fiverr.

Who knows, in the long term you could build your own team of web designers, computer programmers, graphic designers, or translators working on large scale projects across the world!

Other Methods That I Use to Make Money Online

In addition to the 4 methods outlined in this book, I use 2 other ways to generate an online income. Writing books that are published on Amazon (such as this book) and matched betting.

Writing is not covered as there a countless books and internet articles already covering this topic. The aim of this book is to provide the reader with some systems that they may not be aware of and where information is not readily available.

Until recently, matched betting would not have been possible in the US where this book is sold. However, now it is!

No risk matched betting is an incredibly popular method of making money online. It is used by thousands of people throughout the UK and further afield to make a second income. Individuals take advantage of bookmakers' free bets, bonuses, and other promotions in order to make a guaranteed profit. Bookmakers are continually looking for ways to incentivise customers to use their platform. There is a huge range of promotions offered by many different bookmakers across the UK. This makes matched betting a viable source of long term income for those looking to invest a little time and effort.

I am currently in the process of researching US sports betting in order to create a system that provides people in the US the ability to make money in a similar way to no risk matched betting. I shall then be writing a short book covering this topic.

If this is something that may be of interest to yourself, feel free to contact me via email expressing your interest and I shall respond when the book is released on Amazon. Don't worry, your information shall not be passed onto anyone else and I will not send any spam or offers.

stevemacrory@gmail.com

Conclusion

I really hope that this book has been of value to you and I would like to thank you for your purchase. The aim was to summarise all that I have learned over the last 2 years in my quest to make money online. On starting out I would have very much benefited from a guide such as this and I hope that you have found value in what you have read.

If you have found it useful I hope that you can take the time to leave me a quick review on Amazon.

I would like to wish you good luck with your online money making endeavours. Don't give up.

Thanks for reading.

Disclaimer